HOLLY'S AMAZING RESCUE

by

Roger Shinnick

FOREWORD

This book is based on a true story and exemplifies Walkin N Circles Ranch's mission. WNCR exists to rescue, rehabilitate and provide proper care and humane treatment to unwanted, abused and abandoned horses. Its purpose is to provide each rescued horse humane and caring attention in which fear and pain are left at the front gate. Following a total assessment, gentle rehabilitation, training, and a rigorous screening process, WNCR endeavors to find loving adoptive homes for each horse. The objective is to provide each rescued horse a chance for a new start in a useful and productive life.

ISBN-13: 978-0615881874 (Walkin N Circles Ranch, Inc.)

ISBN-10: 0615881874

A Walkin N Circles Rescue Series Book

www.wncr.org

DEDICATION

Holly's story is not unique. Every year there are approximately 170,000 unwanted, abandoned, abused and starved horses in the United States. This book is dedicated to them, as well as to the families and children who want to help, and to the rescues like WNCR that are saving horses every day.

Charles R. Graham
Executive Director
New Mexico Horse Rescue at Walkin N Circles Ranch

CONTENTS

CHAPTER 1 – NEW LIFE

The night sky was filled with stars the summer evening that the mare gave birth to her foal. In the southwest the Big Dipper and other star formations were clearly visible, providing a beautiful backdrop for the miracle of life taking place in an old barn on a prairie in New Mexico.

The foal had a snow white face, a chocolate brown coat, and a stubby black mane and tail. Her body was long and thin. In time she would fill out with the rich milk from her mother.

Both mother and her newborn were resting after the delivery that tired them both. The sweet smelling straw gave them warmth against the cold wind blowing through the cracks in the barn walls.

The mare and her small filly were lying side by side, gazing at one another contentedly. Both giving birth and being born were hard work.

The mare reached over and licked the foal, cleaning her all over. She proudly admired what she had produced. Eleven months of waiting were finally over. The sire was a prized quarter horse who had raced and won many trophies. The mare was so proud knowing that her foal would grow to be big and strong.

But she was worried that she may not have enough milk to feed her hungry baby. The owner had not been generous with the hay when he did the feeding. Luckily, a young ranch hand had secretly given the mare nourishing grain in addition to extra hay, when the boss was not around. He had taken the job at the ranch because he loved horses. But, he had learned that he had to be careful around the boss, who was not kind to the animals.

The foal lifted her head from the sweet smelling straw and nuzzled her mother. Soft sounds came from her mouth as she looked into her mother's gentle, loving eyes.

Just then the young ranch hand came by to check on the mare. He looked down and saw that the foal had already arrived and said. "Well congratulations Helen. You did a great job! Your baby looks very healthy. I brought you some grain to help you get your strength back."

He opened a bag and poured several handfuls of grain into her feed bin. He leaned on the side of the stall and admired the two. The tranquil scene relaxed him before he started his chores. After several minutes he looked at his watch and took off at a run to the farm house. His face turned serious, as he made his way to meet the boss.

The mare stood up so that the foal could nurse. The foal rose to her forelegs on the first try. Her back legs gained their ground next. She stood to get a breath and then wobbled over to her mother. She quickly began to suck from her mother's teet. The warm, sweet milk was soothing.

Their bond was strong. Nothing could hurt them now.

CHAPTER 2 – LOSS

The foal continued to drink the delicious, creamy milk hungrily. Suddenly, both horses heard the barn door open with a bang. The noise also surprised several birds perched in the rafters. They screeched and flew off hurriedly. The young ranch hand returned with his older, weathered boss. They approached the horses' stall with a fourteen-foot lead rope.

The older man yelled at the younger man. "Why did you put the mare in the barn? You know that I sold her. She could have stayed outside and delivered the foal there. You wasted good straw. Besides, I don't plan to keep her foal either."

But, the younger man had learned only minutes earlier that the owner planned to separate the two and sell them as soon as possible. His experience with animals prompted him to object.

"Sir." The younger man said. "She needed to be protected from the high wind. Besides, the dogs might have gotten the foal."

The older man said. "You needn't worry about those mongrels. I locked them up in their pen last night. Listen. If you want to keep your job here, you are going to have to pay more attention to what keeps this place running."

The younger man dared not question the owner again. He needed the job. However, he knew that separating the foal from her mother so soon would mean certain death for the filly.

The mare startled when she saw the whiskered old man peer into the stall with his ugly glare and sour tobacco breath. She vividly remembered his roughness when he handled her before.

The alarm in the mare's body caused the foal to stop nursing again. The mare neighed loudly, flared her nostrils and pawed the ground with her right hoof in defiance. She reached down and moved the foal behind her. If only she could protect her from this man, she thought.

However, the owner reached in and attached the lead rope to the breakaway halter that the mare already wore. The tension in the rope caused the mare to rear up and attempt to strike the older man. The owner yelled at the younger man. "Come over here, so that I can inject her with this drug. If she breaks a leg, I can't sell her."

She could not avoid the injection. The man's grip on the lead rope was too strong. The mare stopped rearing as the drug began to work quickly. She was helpless to protect her foal any longer.

The mare briefly looked at her beautiful baby for the last time, before the younger man opened the stall door and led her out. Her eyes expressed her sadness. She did not want to be separated from her foal. She tried to pull away but she had no strength left. She looked at the younger man, whom she had thought would help her.

The foal was very frightened when the men took her mother away. She did not understand what was going on. Her instinct told her that she should be with her mother. A chill went through her body and she began to shake.

The men walked the mare to the driveway where the horse trailer was waiting. The mare felt woozy and stumbled at the ramp. The owner wasted no time and smacked her hindquarters with a stick saying, "Get in there, you miserable beast!" The sharp pain drove the mare inside, where the owner fastened the rope to a buckle. She was helpless to fight any longer. She knew that she would never see her baby again. Her body sagged in the darkness.

Both men quickly closed the trailer door and jumped into the truck. The sun began to rise in the East as they pulled away.

The buyer had said to be at his farm by eight o'clock with the mare and he would pay the owner eight hundred dollars.

The older man drove with a cigarette hanging from his mouth and a mug of steaming coffee. He sneered at the younger man, saying, "When we get back, I'll take that filly over to Harrison. He offered me two hundred dollars for her. If we are gone only two hours, it won't kill her." The young man kept his gaze ahead on the road in front of them, knowing any comment he could make would be useless.

A strong wind was beating against the sides of the barn causing the splintered wood to flap. The loud sound increased the foal's terror. She did not know what to do. She wobbled as she briefly inspected the straw that still smelled of her mother before she fell down from exhaustion. She neighed hoping that her mother would come back, but there was no response.

Without her mother there to give warmth, the foal became more frightened. The sun had come up lighting the barn. However, it did not brighten her spirits. The pan of water the young man had left for them during the night was still there. She was thirsty and drank from it. However, it did not taste like her mother's milk. She wanted her mom to come back. She neighed again. No sound answered her cry.

The foal fell asleep from the exertion. She dreamt that she was running in a meadow of yellow flowers beside her mother. The birds were chirping, the bees were buzzing, and the nearby brook flowed softly over the smooth rocks. She was so happy to be with her mother and to enjoy the sun's warm rays.

But, this was just a dream.

CHAPTER 3 – RESCUE

Noise erupted on the other side of the ranch where three dogs were fighting over a scrap of meat in their pen. The owner had thrown it in before he left with the mare. He liked to make them fight, so that they would become "good watch dogs." The lead dog had already snatched the fatty piece from the weakest member of the threesome, who was licking his injured front leg.

The leader was chewing on the meat, when the third dog decided to challenge him. Both dogs bared their teeth and let out ferocious growls. The lead dog dropped the meat and attacked the other dog. Their bodies locked in a struggle to inflict serious bites. Their combined weight of over two hundred pounds kicked up dust and debris, as they repeatedly slammed into the sides of the pen. Suddenly, the metal clasps of the pen snapped open on one side and the panel fell away. All three animals stopped, forgot what their battle was about, and quickly leaped to freedom.

The half-starved canines bounded through the pasture looking for a meal. The infrequent feedings from the rancher sent them in search of food. A family of rabbits fled into their burrow and a squirrel darted up a tree when they saw the snarling canines approach.

The dogs' sharp senses picked up a new odor and they sniffed the air excitedly. The scent was coming from the barn. They set off quickly in that direction.

Meanwhile, two miles away, a New Mexico Livestock Board truck was heading toward the ranch. The Board had received complaints about the condition of the horses there, so they had sent an inspector to investigate.

When he arrived, he knocked on the farm house door and then called out. "Hey, is anyone here?" There was no answer. He yelled several more times, but again there was no answer. He looked out in the fields and walked around the property. He could find no one.

The complaint had said that the horses on the ranch looked very thin. He looked across the fence and noted that the horses were indeed so thin that their ribs could be counted. Their heads hung low, and their eyes appeared dull. He wondered why people who kept animals would not care for them.

He snapped several pictures with his digital camera and wrote some notes on the inspection form. The water tanks were green with algae and the corrals clearly had not been mucked for some time. He was upset by what he saw and intended to file his report as soon as he returned to his office. His report would be thorough, so that the county could cite the owner for the deplorable conditions.

He was about to get back into his truck, when he heard dogs growling and cries coming from the barn. He rushed in to see three dogs attacking a smaller animal. The dogs had dragged the animal from the stall leaving a trail of blood. The inspector picked up a stick and chased them away. Returning, he realized that the animal was a newborn foal. Her front legs were badly cut, and her eyes were shut. He thought the horse was already dead, so he went to get a tarp from inside the barn.

But when he returned with the tarp, he was amazed when the foal lifted her head. The inspector was happily surprised and said. "Wow. You poor baby, I thought you were dead. Let's get you out of here!"

The man reached down, scooped up the foal and cradled her in his muscular arms. He ran to his truck with the badly injured foal and laid her gently on a blanket in the enclosed bed. He sped out of the ranch onto to the highway with the tires kicking gravel, then raced to the Western Trails Veterinary Hospital, where he knew they managed such emergencies.

Dark clouds covered the skies as the truck snaked down the highway. The inspector feared the foal wouldn't live.

CHAPTER 4 – RECOVERY

The inspector called ahead, so the veterinary hospital was ready for the injured and unconscious foal. The veterinary staff went to work immediately, giving her fluids and antibiotics and cleaning her wounds.

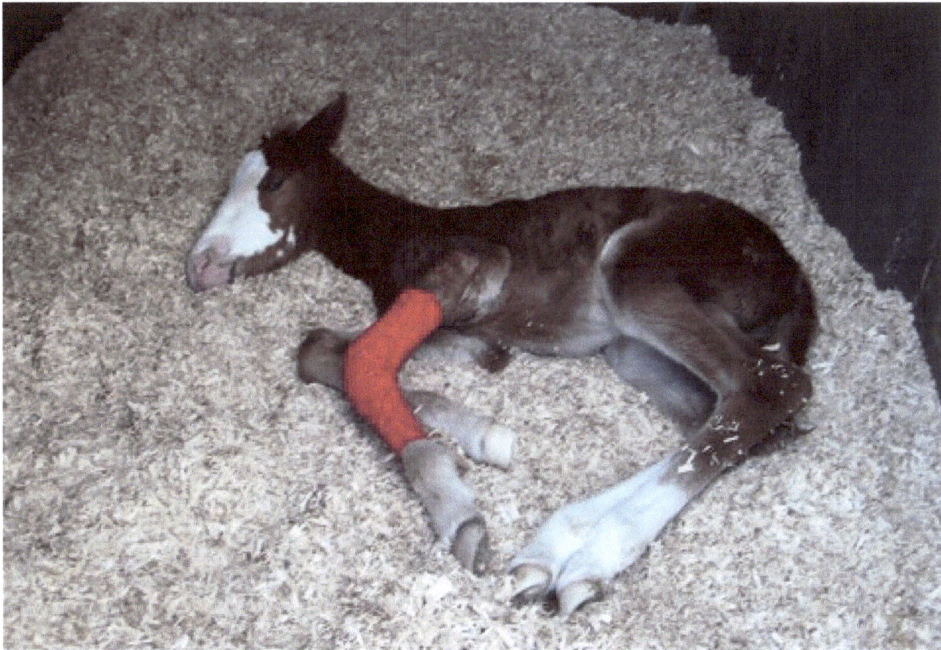

The foal remained unconscious for the rest of the day. The veterinarian and technician, detecting a strong heartbeat, worked feverishly to save her. She was in critical condition due to the lack of nutrition and the extensive injuries from the dog attacks.

The next day there was no change in her condition despite the continuous care from the hospital staff. The veterinarian and technician were deeply concerned, knowing that many animals this young and fragile often did not survive such injuries. They checked on her hourly throughout the day. But, still, there was no change.

It was eight PM and the veterinarian was locking up the hospital for the night, but the tech had not yet put on her coat. "Sally." The veterinarian said. "You need to go home and get some rest. We have two surgeries in the morning and I need you to come in early."

"Doctor." Sally said. "If it is okay with you, I would like to stay here tonight. I have a feeling that our little gal will pull through. I want to be here when she wakes. Then I will be able to feed her super-rich foal formula right away.

"Okay." The veterinarian said. "But, please use the couch in my office and get some sleep. You look as tired as I feel."

Sally went to look at the foal, who was laying quietly amidst the beeps and the flashing lights of emergency equipment that read her vital signs. For now, she was stable. Sally wondered how long it would be before her little friend would wake up, if she would wake up.

The hospital was quiet. Even the cats and dogs recovering from their surgeries were resting peacefully.

There was a baby monitor in the veterinarian's office where Sally lay on a couch. She listened carefully, hoping to hear something from the foal's stall. There was nothing. She fell asleep in spite of her intent to remain alert.

An hour later muffled sounds from the baby monitor awakened Sally. At first she thought she was dreaming, but more sounds told her the foal was awake. She ran to the foal's stall and saw that she was moving her head. The excitement was too much. She yelled. "Yahoooooooooo," which woke up the cats and dogs in the next room. They immediately started meowing and barking and didn't quiet down again for several minutes.

Sally grabbed a phone in the surgical area and called the veterinarian at home. "Doc, guess what? Our little filly is awake! Yes. Yes. I am so happy too! Okay, I'll give her the formula we prepared yesterday. See you soon."

Sally went to the refrigerator, brought out the formula and warmed it in a pan before she transferred it to a baby bottle. She lay down in the stall and held the bottle to the foal's lips. But, the foal rejected the bottle. Sally was heart-broken. She knew the foal had to eat or she would die.

Sally pleaded tearfully, "Come on little gal. You need to eat." But, the foal refused the bottle a second time.

In desperation Sally took out her handkerchief and soaked it in the formula. She brushed the foal's lips with the liquid. Her little pink lips reacted immediately to the change, and the foal immediately began sucking on the cloth hungrily. Sally continued this for five minutes and then decided to pour a little formula in a bowl. This time the foal eagerly began to drink the liquid with sucking noises. Sally held the little filly in her arms. She was so relieved to see the foal eat. Sally felt the foal's heartbeat and smiled. She said to herself. "There is no greater joy in any job than this."

She whispered softly, "Hey, little girl, I think you're going to make it."

The veterinarian showed up thirty minutes later. It was only four AM. She went to the stall and saw both Sally and the little filly lying on the floor. The foal's eyes looked up at Sally with their deep brown color. Sally and the veterinarian looked at each other and laughed about the good news. They were exhausted but happy.

"I guess you were right, Sally." The veterinarian said. "But, you have to understand that she will require continuous care like this for at least another week before we can find her a new home."

"That's not a problem." Sally said. "This little gal deserves the effort. From what the inspector said, she would not have survived if he had not scared the dogs away. She would have been killed."

Sally had studied several courses in school to become a qualified veterinarian technician, but caring for animals was a passion she already had. She stayed every night at the hospital to administer the late feedings and change the filly's dressings. Sally would sit in the make-shift stall and cradle the foal for hours each day. As a result, the foal's condition improved rapidly.

After a few days the veterinarian could not believe her eyes. The foal had responded well to the special attention, the formula and the medication. All vital signs were normal. The veterinarian said. "Sally, you have done a great job with this little filly. You deserve all the credit."

"Thank you, doctor." Sally said. "But, I would not have been able to know how to treat her without the skills I have learned from you at the hospital. I especially love caring for horses."

By the end of the week Sally knew it was time to call Walkin N Circles Ranch, a place that specialized in caring for rescued horses. She wanted to keep the foal longer, but other seriously ill horses were in need of the limited space at the hospital.

Sally made the call and tearfully returned to the little foal's stall. The veterinarian comforted her saying, "Sally, the foal will get excellent treatment at Walkin N Circles. It's what they do, caring for abused and abandoned horses. You can go with me when I go there to follow up."

"Thank you, doctor." Sally said. "I would like that. She is such a cutie, and considering what she has gone through, I would love to be able to watch her grow."

And so she did. Sally had formed a very strong bond with her patient and didn't want to forget her.

CHAPTER 5 – A NEW HOME

The horse trailer sat outside the hospital in the warm sunshine. Walkin N Circles ranch hands were inside signing papers, so that they could take the foal. She was still in her stall, wondering what the commotion was. Sally had just fed her, so the foal expected to go for a walk like on the other days. The foal looked for Sally's return with happy anticipation.

When Sally approached, she held the usual halter and lead rope. So, the foal didn't act surprised until Sally led her toward the trailer. The foal pulled back on the rope and leaned toward the circle pen. The tech came over and stroked her neck and back and said. "Hey, little one, it's time for you to take a trip to a ranch where they will take good care of you. We have done all we can for you here. I know you will like it."

Sally gave her a handful of grain, which the foal ate with pleasure. The friendly stroking and unexpected snack calmed the foal. She even explored the opening of the trailer. The foal smelled the fresh wood shavings and a clean bedspread that had been laid on the floor. With a little coaxing from the tech she walked in.

Sally then invited the two ranch hands from the rescue ranch to enter the trailer and stroke her as well. The three stayed in the trailer for a while, assuring the foal that her temporary quarters would be okay. The foal approved of them by twitching her tail, moving her ears forward and licking her lips.

The foal lay down on the bedspread before the trailer left the hospital. All of the excitement tired her out. She wanted to keep her head up and enjoy the warm rays of sun coming through the window, but she fell asleep. She began to dream of her mother again. She knew that she would never forget her.

An hour later the trailer arrived at Walkin n Circles Ranch, a thirty-five acre spread at the base of the Sandia Mountains. Its buildings and corrals presented a welcome sight for the horses that came there. Several horses looked up curiously as the trailer entered the Ranch gates. Several neighed a welcome to the foal, who was waking up inside the trailer. The morning sun shined radiantly in the bright blue skies.

A team of volunteers was waiting when the trailer pulled up to the barn. They were excited to help the foal get settled in her new surroundings.

The foal picked up her head when the trailer door opened. She expected to see the tech, but instead she saw the man and woman that she had met at the hospital. At first, she was afraid, but the ranch hands calmed her with gentle strokes and soft words. "Ok, little gal, it is time for you to get settled in your new home." She sensed that she could trust them and stopped shaking. One of the two ranch hands cradled her in their arms and got the foal to stand up. After she took a few breaths, she walked out of the trailer and followed them into the barn.

The ranch hands had prepared a stall for her with fresh wood shavings. They wanted her to be as comfortable as she could. The foal was still too weak to be with other horses and needed lots of sleep like all babies. When the ranch hands left the stall, the foal leaned back in the wood shavings and neighed approval.

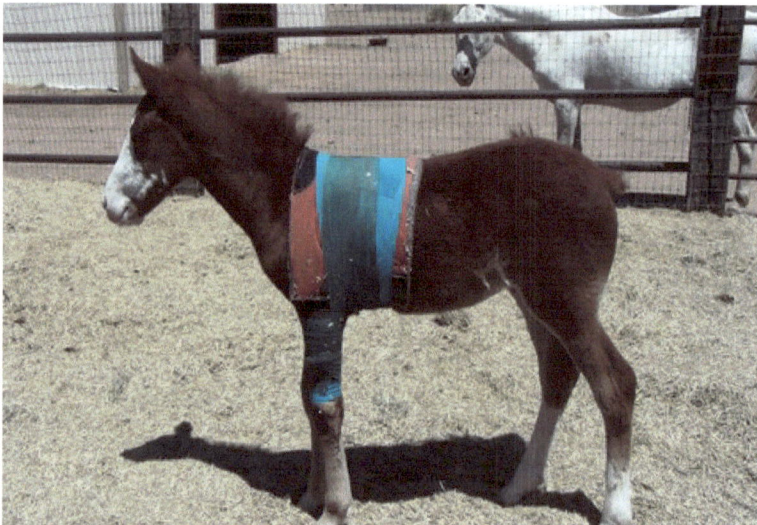

The foal received around-the-clock care for the next two weeks. Four teams of volunteers dedicated themselves to helping with her frequent feedings, medication and change of dressings. She enjoyed the attention and swished her tail when the ranch hands entered her stall.

The foal was finally home.

CHAPTER 6 – HOW THE LITTLE HORSE
GOT HER NAME

The foal made surprising improvement. Her spirits perked up in just a few days. She now stood on her hooves without wobbling. She greeted the ranch hands, who worked with her affectionately. She no longer feared them.

The ranch hands and the veterinarian knew that her recovery was remarkable. They often remarked. "She's a real fighter!" Little did they know that this expression would lead to the name she would be given.

Holly Holm, a professional boxer in Albuquerque, New Mexico, came to the attention of the ranch hands. Holly Holm's success was well known, as a women's boxing world champion. She is considered to be one of the greatest female boxers of all time. After a while the ranch hands started calling the little filly "Holly" after the boxer. Word of the remarkable recovery spread to others outside of the ranch. So, it was no surprise when the foal's success story reached Holly Holm.

Holly Holm visited Walkin N Circles Ranch to meet the little filly who was her namesake. She hung a pair of boxing gloves around the foal's neck for a picture. She recognized how strong Holly the filly was to have survived such an ordeal.

CHAPTER 7 – TRAINING

Six months later Holly had become a good sized filly. The excellent care at the Ranch helped her grow to a healthy weight of three hundred pounds. However, she needed to learn how to be a horse as do all fillies and colts. In the case of Holly, however, the amount of special attention she had received created a more difficult situation. She thought everyone who came into her corral was going to pet and play with her. So she thought she could do whatever she wanted, and she did. The ranch hands put an old mare named Gracie into the corral with her. Gracie had had foals of her own, so she knew how to teach Holly. It wasn't long before Holly tried to test her.

After Holly was fed, she frequently picked up her food bowl and tossed it around like a toy. This was fine with Gracie, so long as Holly didn't touch **her** food bowl, especially when it still had grain or hay in it. She wanted to finish her meal! When

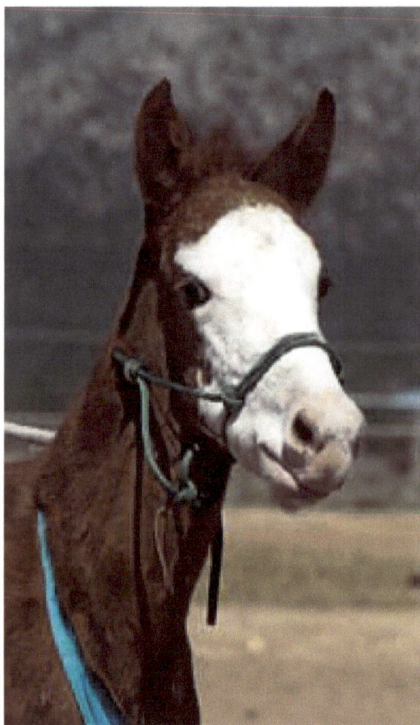

Holly grabbed Gracie's bowl, Gracie was quick to put her hoof in the bowl and hold it down. Holly was no match for Gracie's size and weight.

Holly liked to run in the corral, kicking up her legs and bucking to impress the other horses. Gracie quickly put a stop to this because the close quarters in the corral made Holly's excitement dangerous for both of them. A little nip from Gracie was enough to correct that behavior. Holly wanted Gracie to play with her, but Gracie was a dignified, mature mare and wanted no part of Holly's childish games. Holly learned that the circle pen nearby was the place to frolic and play, and the ranch hands took her there often to run and exercise.

She was happy to stretch her legs and kick up her hooves. The soft sand in the pen even allowed Holly to fall safely, when she took her turns too sharply. She would just get up, shake off the sand and joyfully take off again.

Of course, Holly did not restrict her mischief only to the other horses. She loved to play games with the ranch hands. She would wait patiently while a wheelbarrow was filled with horse droppings. When the ranch hands turned their backs, Holly was right there to tip the wheelbarrow with a kick or a nudge. Holly then walked away, hoping to repeat the fun game again. She did not understand why the ranch hands became grouchy when she did this!

Other times, she would stretch her neck through her upper door opening of her stall and grab halters and ropes hanging on the wall outside on a hook. She would chew the ropes, which helped ease the discomfort of her teething. When that got old, she would drag the gear around the corral much to Gracie's dislike.

When a ranch hand lifted her feet to check the condition of her hooves, she would reach down and nip his or her backside. The ranch hands found the playful nip funny at first, but Holly was developing bad habits that could not be ignored. They would be much more serious when she grew to a weight of over a thousand pounds.

The filly's antics got the attention of the trainers, who decided it was time to teach her needed skills. Holly loved to be stroked and groomed. So, when the ranch hand led her to the circle pen, she said to herself. "Now, I get to play!" But once inside the pen, she soon realized more was expected of her.

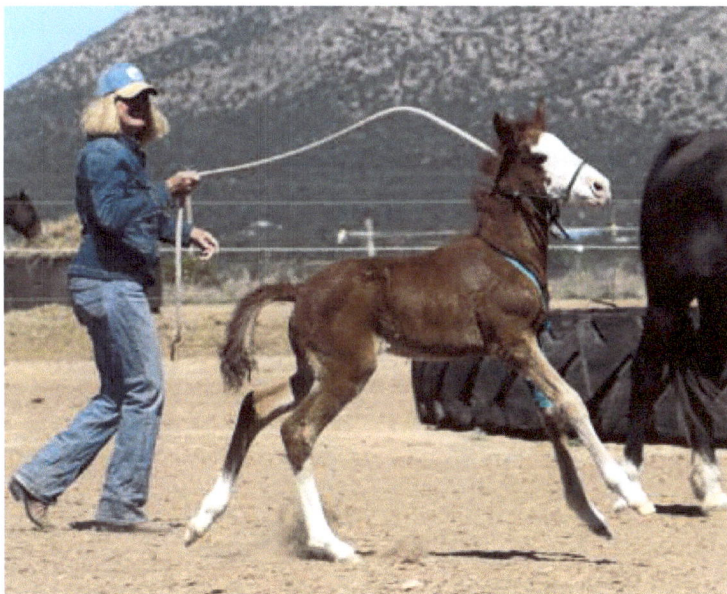

Ranch hand Sharon W. with Holly

Early ground training consisted of a rope being thrown gently on her back. At first, she jumped because no one had done that before. However, she got to like it. It didn't hurt! It actually felt good. The trainer repeated the same action with a training stick. Again, she accepted it. These exercises helped her to learn manners and not be afraid of the training tools.

She liked to walk around the Ranch with the ranch hands. She would look at the other horses like she was saying, "Hey, look at me." The other horses would come up to the fence and look her over. After all, she was new in the neighborhood!

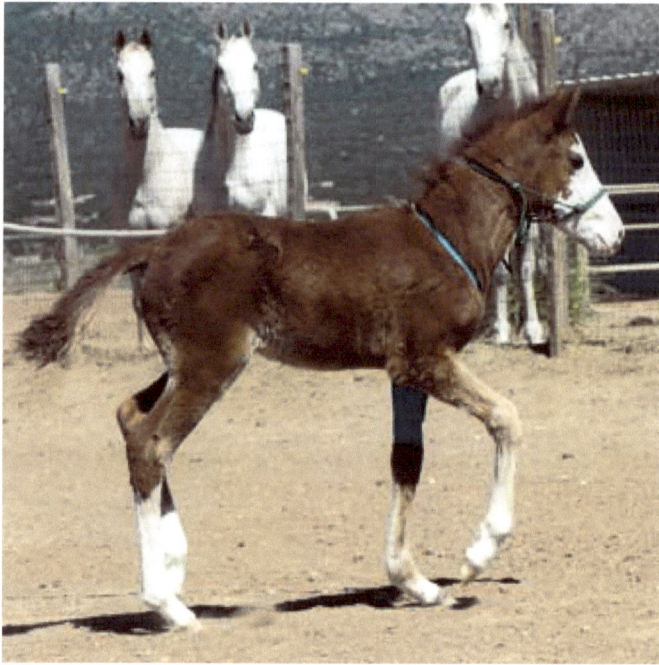

After a few weeks of training, Holly had made good progress. She was learning to be a horse, which made Gracie and the ranch hands happy. The two horses now shared the same corral without incident. Gracie would even lick the ears and side of Holly's head occasionally. In return, Holly would share some of her hay, especially when a sudden wind blew some of Gracie's meal out of the corral.

Holly had not forgotten her mother. But, she was glad she had Gracie to help her become a good horse.

CHAPTER 8 – HOLLY BECOMES A CELEBRITY

Word of Holly's progress spread from the Ranch to the nearby towns. People visited the little filly, which the ranch personnel gladly supported. Holly was happy to see people. She especially liked the children who asked the ranch hands lots of questions like: "How much does she weigh?" "What does she eat?" "Can she run fast?" Holly loved all the attention. She would stand taller when she knew people were talking about her.

Later that year the ranch participated in a parade in Edgewood, New Mexico. Holly rode in a covered wagon that said "Saving Horses with Education." She was the perfect passenger, enjoying the cheering people on the side of the road. Children would yell. "Hey, there is Holly!" Ranch hands stood with her, showing their pride in her too. Holly was glad to be part of the celebration.

She was also featured on a billboard along the state's highways that urged people to report animal cruelty.

In 2013, the Ranch featured Holly in a calendar. Her picture captured her beauty and strength, and allowed her to stand out as one of the wonderful animals the Ranch saves daily.

CHAPTER 9 – HOLLY BECOMES A MARE

Today, Holly continues to live at the Walkin N Circle Ranch, where she has become a strong and mature mare. Her advancement came about because the NM Livestock Board, Western Trails Veterinary Hospital, and WNCR cared enough to rescue, nurture and care for her.

Holly's training required ranch hands to devote years of dedicated service, so that she could master the critical movements that make a horse a reliable animal for riding and other enjoyment. WNCR used gentle training techniques for her to overcome fear and accept people as trustworthy.

If you were to visit Holly, you would see her standing expectantly, a strong, healthy horse, grown to be a deserving partner to a horse lover and rider. She is ready to go to her forever home with a family, who will love and care for her.

Holly's story is an incredible one, where even with a horrible beginning by a cruel and thoughtless person, there is hope provided by horse rescues around the country. These remarkable places are taking a sad beginning for many horses and turning it into a new start in a useful, productive and loving life.

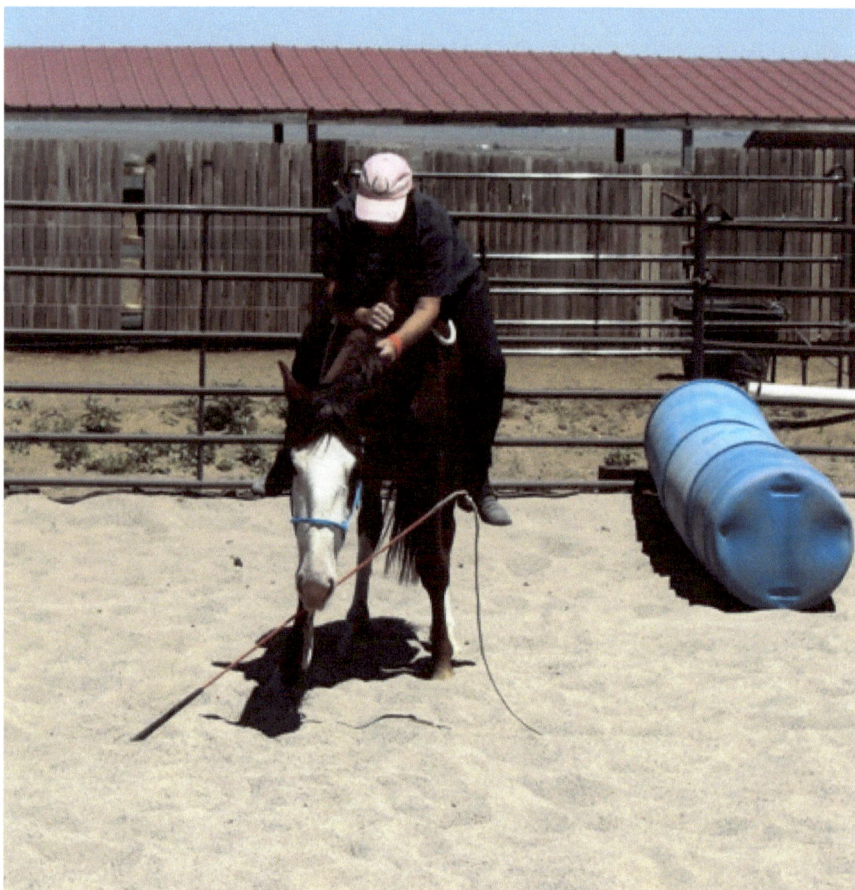

Didi A., with Holly under saddle, picking up a stick

EPILOGUE

WNCR, Inc. is a Registered 501(c)3 Non-Profit organization, certified by the New Mexico State Livestock Board as a New Mexico Horse Rescue. If you would like more information, please write, call or email as follows: P.O.Box 626, Edgewood, NM 87015, (505) 286-0779, www.wncr.org.

Walkin N Circles is only one of hundreds of horse rescue ranches in the United States. More information on the location and activity of these other horse rescues can be obtained from the internet.

BIBLIOGRAPHY

The Humane Society of the United States. "Relinquishing Your Horse." 26 Feb 2013. <http://www.humansociety.org/animals/horses/tips/relinquishing_your_horse.html>

Walkin N Circles. "Ranch Handbook." 2012. <http://www.wncr.org> 26 February 2013.

www.ingramcontent.com/pod-product-compliance
Lightning Source LLC
LaVergne TN
LVHW072052070426
835508LV00002B/67